32 Mistakes To Avoid When You Sell Your Business

Ben Hill

ISBN: 978-0-578-69635-5

DEDICATION

This book is dedicated to all of my clients. Your hard work and risk taking inspires me. The trust you place in me is humbling and motivating. I would not be where I am today without you. Thank you.

CONTENTS

INTRODUCTION

Become CEO Over Your Selling Process

We often learn best when we make mistakes. Mistakes can hurt, but they can also be our best teachers. The goal of this book is to know the mistakes before you make them. If you know the mistakes ahead of time, you can avoid making them.

I believe if you use this book to its fullest potential it will help you be a competent "CEO" over the process of selling your company. Afterall, if you are not looking out for your best interests in the sale of your business, who is?

You may have your CPA, attorney and business broker working on your behalf in the sale of your business, but at the end of the day, no one can look out for your interests better than you. In fact, your tendency to look out for yourself is one of the reasons you have been a successful business owner in the first place.

It only makes sense for you to take this same mentality into the sale of your business by becoming a competent "CEO over your selling process". This is my goal for you. If you read this book, I am very confident this will become true for you.

By reading this book, you will better understand the process of selling your business, what players are involved (buyers, attorneys, CPAs, banks, etc.) and where the mistakes occur.

Then, when it comes time to sell your business, you will be prepared to go through the process with less anxiety, fewer mistakes and more advantages during and after the deal is done.

Who This Book Is For

This book is for small business owners. For the purposes of this book, you are a small business owner if your business has between zero dollars to twenty million dollars in sales per year. If this is you, you are in the right place.

If you own a business, you know more than anything that life is busy. You probably do not have a lot of extra time in your day for things like reading books about selling your business.

I have written this book with your limited time in mind. I try to keep the writing in this book "short and sweet". I take a "tell it like it is" approach because this tends to be what business owners appreciate the most. You just don't have time to sift through lots of words and sentences. You need me to get right to the point and that is what I do in this book.

How To Read This Book

This book consists of 32 mistakes that are grouped into 5 categories based on the type of mistake: Mistakes Involving Financials, Mistakes Involving Buyers, Mistakes Involving Timing, Mistakes Involving Deal Making and Mistakes Involving Business Brokers.

I have also included a chapter titled "The Selling Process" that will help you have a better understanding of the overall process of selling your business.

I have written this book so that you can either read it start to finish or use it as a point of reference where you read the mistakes that are most interesting to you regardless of their order in this book. In other words, you don't have to read this book in any particular order for it to make sense.

THE SELLING PROCESS

You may be curious to know what the process for selling your business will involve. Below I break the selling process down into 5 steps:

Step 1: Preparation

- Prepare your past 3 years financial statements and tax returns for your business. Work with a CPA if you need help doing this.
- If you plan to use a business broker to sell your business, interview 2-3 business brokers.
- Have a CPA or business broker perform a valuation of your business in order to determine what your initial asking price will be for your business.

Step 2: Find Buyers and Disclose Information

- You or your business broker will find buyers and screen them to make sure they are qualified.
- You must have qualified buyers sign an NDA before sharing confidential information about your business with them.
- Disclose a reasonable amount of information about your business to buyers as they ask for it.

Step 3: Negotiation and Offer Acceptance

- The buyer submits their initial offer.
- You and the buyer negotiate directly or through your business broker.
- If the negotiation leads to an agreement, you sign accepting the buyer's offer.

Step 4: Due Diligence

- Once you accept the buyer's offer, due diligence begins.
- Due diligence usually lasts 30-45 days.

- During due diligence the buyer (and their bank if they are getting a loan to buy your business) reviews much more detailed information about your business to confirm that the claims that you made about your business are indeed true.
- Your attorney and the buyer's attorney will work on the Purchase Agreement for the transaction along with any other relevant legal documents depending on what your transaction requires.

Step 5: Closing

- Once due diligence is completed and the Purchase Agreement and other legal documents are finalized, the closing takes place on an agreed upon date and time.
- After closing, the sale of your business is now complete.

Now that you have a better idea of the overall process for selling your business, let's take a look at the mistakes that can happen during this process so that you can avoid making them.

MISTAKES INVOLVING FINANCIALS

MISTAKE #1: THINKING YOU CAN SELL YOUR BUSINESS WITHOUT SHOWING TAX RETURNS

You tell buyers that your business makes a certain amount of sales and profit every year. You even show buyers financial statements, reports and other documents to prove it.

But, how do buyers know that the statements and documents you give them aren't fake?

Buyers will review the tax returns for your business.

Additionally, if the buyer is getting a loan from a bank to buy your business their bank will get the tax returns for your business directly from the IRS via a release (IRS Form 4506-T) that you sign giving the IRS your permission.

Buyers and their banks want to make sure that these tax returns line up with the financial statements for your business.

Often the tax returns are different from the financial statements for your business. If this is the case, then buyers will require you to show the reconciliation of these differences using proper documentation. You should work with your CPA to produce this documentation. Often this documentation is called "Accountant's Working Papers".

If you want to sell your business, you will have to show buyers and their banks tax returns for your business. There is no way around this, so be ready.

MISTAKE #2:
THINKING YOU CAN SELL YOUR BUSINESS WITHOUT SHOWING FINANCIAL STATEMENTS

The first things buyers ask for are the financial statements for your business. This is what buyers care about the most.

The financial statements for your business are:

- Profit and Loss Statement (also called Income Statement)
- Balance Sheet
- Statement of Cash Flows

Buyers will want to see these financial statements for the current year and 2 years prior. If you do not give buyers these statements after they sign the NDA, you may have a hard time selling your business.

Buyers will definitely get the tax returns for your business. But these tax returns may not give them enough detail on the expenses of your business. Buyers are not going to spend a bunch of their money buying your business if they don't understand what the expenses of your business are. After all, when the buyer owns your business, they will be responsible for all these expenses just as you are today.

If you do not have financial statements for your business, work with a CPA to create them. Working with a CPA will take time and cost money, but it is probably a necessity for you at this point. If you haven't already done your financial statements yourself, you probably won't be able to do them yourself now either. Let's face it, you need the help of a CPA to get this done.

MISTAKE #3: CHANGING YOUR FINANCIAL STATEMENTS BASED ON ASSUMPTIONS YOU MAKE ABOUT BUYERS

When buyers ask for the financial statements for your business give them the complete financial statements. Do not give them financial statements that you have modified.

For example, if the buyer is going to use their current office staff to run your business after they buy it, do not remove the salaries for your office staff from the expenses of your financial statements. It may be tempting to do this, and you could justify it to yourself saying, "Well, they'll be using their own office staff so they can use their own numbers for that". Do not make this mistake. If you do, you may very well hurt the trust you have built with that buyer when they find out all of your expenses when they review the tax returns for your business during due diligence.

But what if you change your financial statements and you tell the buyer that you changed them? From the example above, you might say to the buyer "Here are my profit and loss statements and I want to let you know I removed the salaries expenses for my office staff since you will be using your current office staff". Do not do this! Again, it goes back to trust. Even if you tell the buyer about the changes you made to the financial statements, the buyer may wonder what other expenses you have changed or removed and not told them about.

Just give buyers your complete financial statements and let the buyers make their own adjustments to the statements as they see fit. This will build trust between you and the buyer and make it more likely that you will strike a deal.

Remember, the buyer will eventually find out all of your expenses on your tax returns during due diligence. There is nowhere to hide. It is best to be up front and disclose your full and complete financial statements the first time buyers ask for them.

Besides, if you do not like the offer the buyer makes after they review your full and complete financial statements, you do not have to accept it. You can respectfully explain to the buyer why your business is worth more than they have offered even though your financial statements are what they are.

MISTAKE #4: NOT KNOWING WHAT MAKES YOUR BUSINESS VALUABLE TO BUYERS

What is most valuable to buyers? The answer is simple: Profit.

Your equipment, your brand, your real estate, and many more things may or may not be valuable to buyers. But, if your business is making a profit and this profit is not likely to go down to zero anytime soon, that is going to be valuable to buyers because it gives them a return on their investment.

It is important that you know what a buyer thinks is valuable about your business and what they do not think is valuable. This will increase your chances of reaching an agreement with a buyer because you will both be on the same page about what is valuable about your business.

For example, let's say you owned a company that performs services for customers. You might think your equipment is valuable. But the buyer might think your equipment can easily be bought from several different equipment dealers in your area. The buyer might think how efficiently your employees perform the services of your business is more valuable than your equipment.

If you and the buyer are not on the same page about what is valuable, then you may have difficulty agreeing on what your business is worth. In the example above, the buyer will be focusing on how efficient your services are when they think about what price they will pay for your business, but you will be focusing on how much all of your equipment is worth as you think about how much money you want to get for the sale of your business. The end result is that you and the buyer may be far off from each other when it comes to what price your business deserves.

To help you know what is valuable about your business, here is a breakdown of some of the different parts of a business into three categories based on value: Almost Always Valuable, Usually Valuable and Maybe Valuable.

What Is Almost Always Valuable

- Profit: Profit gives buyers a return on their investment. Profit is money that buyers believe they can take home at the end of the day. If the profit your business generates is not expected to go to zero anytime soon, it is valuable.

What is Usually Valuable

- Customer List: Your customer list is usually valuable because it could mean more easy sales in the future. What makes a customer list especially valuable is if your sales are not concentrated on a short list of clients, but instead your sales are spread out across many different clients. This topic is called "customer concentration". Buyers prefer that your sales are not concentrated on a short list of customers because if one or two of your top clients leave, your business will not lose too many sales as a result.
- Employees: Your team of employees that will remain with your company after you sell it are usually considered valuable to buyers because as the saying goes "good help is hard to find". If these employees have been with the company a long time and plan to stay after the buyer takes over, then buyers may consider them even more valuable.
- Patents and Proprietary Assets: If you have patents and proprietary assets such as proprietary software or processes and they are still a key to you maintaining your share of your market or industry, then these are also usually considered valuable by buyers.
- Suppliers: Your relationships and contracts that you have with your suppliers are usually considered valuable by buyers because you have already done the hard work of getting them established and taken the risk of trying out a new supplier to make sure they do a good job. If the supplier relationships that you have are hard to find, then this increases their value even more.

What Is Maybe Valuable

- Equipment: If your equipment is not highly specialized or customized, but is readily available in the marketplace, then this equipment is only valuable in as much as your entire company is valuable. In other words, if the operation of your company is not valuable in terms of profit or sales then buyers are not any more interested in buying your equipment compared to the next equipment dealer down the street or in the next town over. On the other hand, if highly specialized or customized equipment is used by your business and is difficult to find in the marketplace, then even if your company is not making a profit this equipment still may be valuable.

- Inventory: Your inventory may or may not be valuable in and of itself. Inventory can be sold in a business transaction as a separate line item in the total deal, but it will generally not be for more than cost and could even be for a fraction of cost. The exceptions to this would be if you have rare inventory that is not readily available elsewhere in the marketplace. In these cases, your inventory may be included in the transaction of your business for a value higher than cost.
- Real Estate: When it comes to the success of your business your real estate may or may not be valuable. The key question you need to ask is: Could my business achieve the same level of success if it were located somewhere else? For example, if your business could be run successfully from any office building or warehouse, then your real estate does not add value to the success of your business operation. On the other hand, if your restaurant, store or dealership is located in a great location, then your real estate may add value to the success of your business operation. As you can see, this is not a question of whether or not your real estate is valuable just for the sake of real estate. This is a question of whether or not your real estate adds to the value of the operation of your business...does your real estate play a key role in how much sales and profit your business makes or could you make the same sales and profits from another location? Likewise, people who are buying businesses are not buying your business only for the real estate. If that were the case, they would be buying your real estate, not your business! People who are buying businesses are first are foremost buying a successful operation and your real estate may or may not be essential to the success of this operation.
- Brand: The fact that you may have spent thousands of dollars on creating a name and logo for your business, does not mean that these things are valuable. The biggest factor that determines if your brand adds extra value to your business is simply how long you have been in business for. If you have been in business for 10, 20, 30+ years and your customer base is still as full as it has ever been then buyers may view your brand as valuable. On the other hand, if your business is not profitable or your sales are in decline, buyers may not view your brand as being valuable enough to make up for these sales and profit deficits.

Now that you have a better idea of what buyers think is valuable and what is not you will have a better chance of getting on the same page with a buyer and reaching an agreement to sell your business. If you and the buyer have different ideas about what is valuable in your business, the chances that you will reach an agreement are small. If you start to have several buyers who do not share your opinion of what parts of your business are valuable and what parts are not, it may be time to refer back to this section of this book and reassess your thinking on what makes a business valuable to buyers.

MISTAKE #5:
THINKING YOUR BUSINESS IS WORTH MORE THAN IT REALLY IS

Do you have a number in mind that you want to sell your business for? How did you come up with this number?

Maybe you own a great business that makes a nice profit and you've always dreamed of selling your company for a certain amount of money when you retire.

On the other hand, maybe your business is not doing that good, but you have a business loan and you would like to sell your business so that you can pay back the loan.

No matter how you came up with the number that you want to sell your business for, you have to ask yourself: Is this number realistic?

If your number is unrealistic you will probably end up wasting a lot of your time, energy and maybe even your money trying to sell your business for a price that you will never get.

How do you know if your number is realistic? You should get 2-3 opinions of what your business is worth from CPAs and business brokers. CPAs and business brokers should be willing to do a basic valuation of your business for you either for free or minimal cost.

MISTAKE #6:
ACCEPTING LESS MONEY FOR YOUR BUSINESS THAN YOU SHOULD

You may have an employee, a friend or a family member who wants to buy your business. The offer they make you may seem fair, but is it really? What if your business is actually worth a lot more?

With all the hard work and sacrifices you have made you owe it to yourself and your family to get a fair price for your business. If someone you know is interested in buying your business the first step is to have an unbiased third party such as a CPA or business broker perform a valuation on your business.

Valuations are easy to do and should only take a few days if done by a CPA or business broker. The CPA or business broker should either do it for free or at most charge you around $300 because the valuation report should be simple—only 1 or 2 pages long. You do not need every penny in your business to be accounted for in the valuation. Just a general idea or even a range of what your business is worth is all you are looking for.

Once you receive your valuation report and you know what your business is really worth then you can have a fair discussion with that employee, friend or family member about striking a deal together.

Keep in mind that if your business is worth more than your employee, friend or family member thinks they can afford you may still be able to make a deal that will work using what is called "seller financing".

With seller financing you essentially function as the buyer's bank because you give ownership of your business to the buyer at closing and then after the closing the buyer pays you in monthly payments over time.

To learn more about the different types of payments buyers use to pay you see Mistake #21: Not being realistic about your deal structure.

MISTAKE #7: NOT ACCEPTING THAT YOUR BUSINESS IS UNSELLABLE

Your business may be unsellable. This means that most likely no one is going to buy it. Businesses are usually unsellable for one or more of the following reasons:

Reason #1
The business does not make enough profit.

Reason #2
The business makes a profit, but the profit is decreasing, will be zero within 3-5 years and this can't be fixed.

Reason #3
The sales of the business are decreasing, will be zero within 3-5 years and this can't be fixed.

If your business is unsellable because of Reason #2 or Reason #3, your business will probably never be sellable. One example of this is when an industry is rapidly transformed by technology making your entire business model obsolete and you have no ability to adopt the new technology into your business. Maybe a few companies in your industry created software that now does what you do at a fraction of the cost. Unless you can build similar software, you will most likely be out of business before long and there is no way to fix this.

If your business is unsellable because of Reason #1, there is still hope that you can sell your business down the road. However, do not try to sell your business right now. You need to work on your business so that it makes a sufficient amount of profit for at least 1-2 years before you try to sell it.

For the purpose of determining if a business is sellable sufficient profit is defined as at least a 5% EBITDA margin. EBITDA is commonly used in financial analysis and stands for earnings before interest, taxes, depreciation and amortization. Be aware that while a 5% EBITDA margin is the minimum for determining if a business is sellable, most buyers want an EBITDA margin of 10% or greater.

If you move forward and try to sell your business when it is unsellable you can expect to waste a lot of time, energy and maybe even money. Selling a business is a time-intensive and tedious process. You will be doing conference calls and meetings with buyers and soon as they see your financial statements they will walk away. You are just wasting your time.

If your business is unsellable, do not live in denial. You need to accept reality and proceed accordingly.

There is one important exception that must be considered when it comes to determining if your business is unsellable: Would one of your competitors like to buy you?

If one of your competitors is interested in acquiring your business your sales and profits may be mostly irrelevant. It all depends on your competitor. Your competitor may be content to buy you for other reasons besides your sales and profits. They may be interested in acquiring your: Customer list, team of employees, location, specialized equipment or your brand.

If this is the case, then you still may be able to sell your business to one of your competitors even though your business is unsellable to all other buyers.

MISTAKE #8: NOT DOING PERSONAL TAX PLANNING BEFORE YOU LIST YOUR BUSINESS FOR SALE

The sale of your company may have an impact on your personal taxes. Do not wait until it is too late to do tax planning.

The time to determine what the impact might be is before you start the process of selling your company. There may be opportunities during the selling process to reduce your tax liability related to the sale. If you are not prepared in advance you might miss these opportunities.

One common example of this type of opportunity from the past is the IRS 1031 Exchange. But the tax code is always changing, and your CPA should be up to date on all of the current opportunities in the tax codes that you might be able to take advantage of.

Everyone's personal tax situation can be different so you need to meet with your CPA to determine what the impact of a sale may be on your specific situation.

Being prepared in advance gives you the best chance to minimize your tax liability when opportunities arise during the selling process. This could potentially save you a lot of money when you sell your business.

MISTAKES INVOLVING BUYERS

MISTAKE #9:
NOT SCREENING BUYERS ENOUGH

Just because someone is interested in buying your business does not mean they are a good fit. Your time is limited. You do not have time to share information about your business with every buyer that shows an interest.

You should screen buyers to make sure they have the money to buy your business. No matter how much they like your business and how much you like them, if they don't have the money, they can't buy it.

Buyers should also be screened to make sure they have the experience and personality to run your business. For example, a buyer might be really interested in your business and they may have plenty of money to buy it. However, this buyer's past career experience may consist of working behind a desk from 9am-5pm Monday-Friday. And one of the things your business would involve is the buyer driving a forklift to load semi-trucks for 12 hours every Saturday.

Does it make sense to spend your time sharing information about your business with this buyer? Maybe, maybe not. In this example you should ask the buyer if they realize that they would be driving a forklift for 12 hours every Saturday. You would want to get assurance from the buyer that they are willing to do what is required to run the business before you move forward and spend lots of time sharing information about your business with them.

Buyers may daydream about owning your business, but when the time comes for them to put their money on the line and buy it they will inevitably get cold feet if they have not faced all the realities, both good and bad, about your business.

You have a limited amount of time. You only want to spend time on buyers that are a good fit and that have enough money to buy your business. If you do not screen buyers enough you will end up wasting a lot of time and energy.

You could have spent this valuable time and energy on something else like running your business! Make sure your business does not suffer because you are spending too much of your time and attention talking to buyers that will never buy your company.

MISTAKE #10: NOT USING AN NDA

NDA stands for Non-Disclosure Agreement. An NDA is a legal document a potential buyer signs before learning about your business. The NDA prohibits the buyer from sharing information about your business or the fact that it is even for sale with other people.

Always require buyers to sign an NDA before you share information with them about your business even if you think a buyer can be trusted. Do not take the risk of your clients or employees finding out you are selling the company. If this happens, clients may decide to take their business to your competition and your best employees may decide to leave out of fear for their job security under new owners.

No matter how well you know the buyer, they must sign an NDA--no exceptions.

If you do not even want the buyer to know your name or the name of your business before they sign the NDA you can have your attorney or business broker execute the NDA with them with you as the anonymous third party beneficiary to the agreement.

MISTAKE #11: BEING SLOW TO RESPOND TO BUYER INFORMATION REQUESTS

Buyers will request that you share a lot of information with them. They will want to see financial information, operations information, equipment information, sales information and much more.

When the buyer makes a specific information request it is important to respond quickly because it shows the buyer that your business is organized and that you have nothing to hide. A fast response shows them you are eager to share information with them because you know you have a great business.

This is especially important when it comes to providing buyers with your financial information. If you are slow to respond when the buyer requests financial information buyers will think you are not organized. Even worse they may start to doubt if your financial information can be trusted. They will wonder why it took so long to send your financial information—did you have to spend time making up fake numbers?

You should have your financial statements for the current year to date and the previous 2 years finished and ready to send to buyers before you list your company for sale. You should also have your other records and reporting systems up to date and ready for buyer information requests prior to listing your business for sale.

MISTAKE #12: BEING EVASIVE

When a buyer asks you a direct question such as "Why did your net profit margin decrease last year?", give them a direct answer. Do not be evasive by trying to talk your way around hard questions or subtly change the topic when it suits you.

For example, don't answer a question like the one above with "Last year was tough, we had a lot of growth in areas we didn't expect, but there were also some areas that were harder. But, this year we're already ahead of where we expected to be." This is an example of an evasive answer and buyers do not like this.

Instead, one example of how to give a direct answer to the question above would be: "Our net profit margin decreased last year because we expanded our team by adding a new customer service person and a new office manager."

Buyers are considering taking on a lot of personal risk to buy your company and when they ask you a direct and specific question, they expect a direct and specific answer.

If you don't know the answer to a buyer's question, it is perfectly fine to say, "I don't know." Saying "I don't know" is better than being evasive.

If the buyer asks you a question about one of the weak points of your business, do not avoid the question. Answer their question honestly even if it is a weak spot for your business.

The reason you should answer buyers' questions directly and honestly is that buyers will eventually uncover the truth during due diligence before you can close the sale with them.

In our example above where you give an evasive answer to the question of why your net profit margin decreased last year, the buyer will review your payroll records during due diligence and be able to easily see that you increased the size of your team by 2 full time employees.

There is nowhere to hide in due diligence. The buyer will review everything about your business in detail.

It is much better to be up front than to make the buyer figure it out for themselves during due diligence. If buyers have to figure out the truth for themselves later on in the process during due diligence, they will lose faith and trust in doing a deal with you and may even back out of the deal all together.

Answer buyers' questions honestly and directly. Doing this will save you time, embarrassment and heartache because buyers will uncover the truth eventually and when they do, they may say goodbye for good.

MISTAKE #13:
TALKING TOO MUCH ABOUT WHAT COULD BE

It's true. When buyers look at your business, they think about what their future might be like if they owned it.

But, make no mistake, when a buyer actually decides to buy your business it is not because of what your business could be in the future, it is because of what your business has been in the past.

When it comes time for the buyer to take the risk and put their money on the table at closing or sign on the dotted line for that loan from the bank, they are doing it based on how your business performed in the past under your ownership because past performance is much more certain than what the business might do in the future. The past is certain, we know what happened in the past. None of us know what the future holds.

Buyers are interested to hear what you have to say about the past performance of your business. They are not interested in hearing your thoughts on what the business could be. If you talk more about what your business could become in the future than you do about what it has been in the past under your ownership, it either goes in one of the buyer's ears and out the other or worse the buyer becomes suspicious that they are being sold a lot of hype and that the business in its current state must not be that great otherwise you would be talking about the past and the present as opposed to the future.

You should talk more about what you wished you would had done differently in the past with your business than what a new owner could do after buying the business. If you make the mistake of talking too much about what your business could be, buyers will start to ask themselves why you haven't gone ahead and done it yourself while you owned it.

MISTAKE #14: THINKING GOOD SALES AND MARKETING WILL GET YOUR BUSINESS SOLD

When it comes to selling your business, being a skilled salesperson and having a good marketing presentation will not make a difference as to whether or not your business sells and at what price.

That's right, I said it won't make a difference.

Buyers are not interested in buying your business because of how great your presentation for selling your business is. They are interested in buying your business because it is going to make them money. The past performance of your business that is recorded in your financial statements and tax returns speaks for itself on this matter.

In fact, the more you try to persuade buyers to buy your business with your sales skills and the fancier your marketing presentation for selling your business is, the more suspicious buyers become. It appears to buyers that you are trying to use your sales and marketing skills to hide the fact that your business is weak.

Buyers just want the facts. They want accurate information about your business. Do not try to "sell" them on your business. Get out of the way and let the facts of your business speak for themselves. Let your business sell itself.

If your business is not doing well and you are afraid to let the facts speak for themselves, I recommend you read the "Mistakes Involving Financials" section of this book to see if it is possible for you to plan a course of action to correct your current situation.

MISTAKES INVOLVING TIMING

MISTAKE #15: TRYING TO SELL YOUR BUSINESS TOO SOON

Have you owned your business for 2 years or less? If so, and your sales or profits have decreased by 10% or more under your ownership, it may be hard to sell your business right now.

The combination of short time of ownership and decreasing sales or profits makes buyers worry that you've uncovered a serious problem with your business, and you are trying to get out before the business fails.

On the other hand, if you have owned your business for 2 years or less and your sales and profits have not decreased by 10% or more during this time, you may be able to sell even though you have not owned it for very long. For example, buyers may be willing to accept that you have developed a medical issue or have realized you do not like the lifestyle of your business as much as you thought you would.

If you fall into the first category and you have owned your business for 2 years or less and your sales or profits have decreased during this time by 10% or more, do not make the mistake of trying to sell your business right now. Most likely no one is going to buy it and you will be wasting your valuable time and energy trying to sell it. Your best bet is to invest this time and energy into your business for 2-3 more years until you can demonstrate stable or increasing sales and profits and then try to sell at that point. If you feel that your business is not worth 2-3 more years of your time and energy, why would a buyer feel that it is worth it to spend 2-3 years of their time and energy on your business, not to mention their money buying your business?

MISTAKE #16: WAITING TOO LONG TO SELL YOUR BUSINESS

You know from experience that the longer you own a business the faster each year goes by. Before you know it maybe even decades have gone by.

Do not wait too long to sell your business. Even though you are busy, take time now to plan when you will leave your business.

And do not only think about your personal finances when deciding when to sell. Also think about your health.

For example, your personal financial plan might call for you to run your business for 4 more years in order for your nest egg to be the size you prefer for retirement. However, in year 2 of the last 4 years you develop a medical condition and, as a result, your business performance suffers during the remaining 2 years that you own it. As a result of the decrease in performance of your business in the last 2 years, you end up selling your business for 35% less than you could have if you would have sold it 4 years sooner. Is this 35% loss in sale price more than the money you put towards your retirement nest egg during the last 4 years that you owned your business? If so, you would have been better off selling 4 years ago and starting retirement 4 years sooner!

This is the type of question you need to ask yourself as you think about when to sell your business. Don't wait too long to ask yourself these questions.

What if you don't have any medical concerns and your business has been doing so well that you already have the nest egg that you need for retirement saved? Or what if you are not close to retirement age, but want to eventually move on to your next venture? Is it still possible to wait too long to sell?

The answer is yes, it is still possible to wait too long to sell your business. Buyers will look at the last 3-5 years of financial performance of your business. If the sales or profits of your business have been in steady decline during the last 3-5 years, you will get less for your business than you could have if you would have sold 3-5 years sooner. Some business owners "take their foot off the gas" and stop growing their businesses towards the final years of ownership. You may get tired, bored or decide that you have more than enough money to support your lifestyle and do not need to continue to hustle to boost sales in the final years of owning your business. If this is you, beware that each year of decrease in sales or profits will mean a decrease in the amount of money you will get when you sell your business. What this means is that you may be better off going ahead and selling your business now rather than continuing to own your business while it is in decline for 3-5 more years. Once again, do the math, would you rather continue to get 3-5 more years of profits or would you rather get a higher price when you sell your business. Perhaps it is time to start your retirement or your next business venture now, not 3-5 years from now.

No matter what your situation is you need to set aside some time now to plan when you will sell your business. If you don't the years will continue to sneak by you and before you know it, it will be too late and you will have to try to quickly sell your business because of a medical condition or because your business has declined to a point that it has lost a majority of the value that it once had when it was in its prime.

Set aside 30 minutes this week on your calendar and start to plan when you want to sell your business. You will be glad you spent 30 minutes this week rather than losing unnecessary years and significant amounts of money if you would have not made a plan and waited too long to sell your business.

MISTAKE #17: THINKING YOUR BUSINESS WILL SELL QUICKLY

Be aware for your planning purposes that businesses usually take a while to sell. Even if your business makes a nice profit every year and you are asking a low price for it, it could still end up taking 12 months or more to sell it.

Selling a business is a slow process. You have to find buyers that are worth talking to, review a lot of information with them, put together a deal that you both agree on, and, if the buyer is getting a loan, their bank will move slowly. All of this adds up. The selling process takes time. You will not be able to sell your business quickly, so you need to plan accordingly.

When do you want to be done with your business? You should put your business on the market at least 12 months prior to this date.

Make sure you have at least 3 years of past financial statements ready to send to buyers before you put your business on the market. If you need to work with your CPA to get these financial statements ready, add the additional time this takes to the 12-month minimum time frame.

MISTAKE #18: NEGLECTING YOUR BUSINESS AFTER YOU PUT IT UP FOR SALE

You just learned in Mistake #17 that even the best businesses can end up taking 12 months or more to sell. This means that your business will continue to report financial performance while it is on the market for sale. Do not "kick back and put your feet up" while your business is on the market or it could come back to bite you.

Let me give you an example. Let's say that your business had its best year ever last year and you decide to put it on the market for sale. Even though your business makes a great profit and is very sellable it ends up taking 12 months from the time you first listed it for sale to the time you found the right buyer who made the right offer. Now 12 months after you first listed your business for sale the buyer's bank is reviewing your financial statements as a standard part of their due diligence to determine whether or not they are going to loan the buyer money to buy your business. It is at this point that the bank says to you "We only have your financial statements for the previous 4 years; can you please send us your financial statements for the last 12 months that just ended!"

If you neglected your business over the last 12 months while your business was for sale your financial performance—your sales and profits—may have decreased during this time. If this is the case, the buyer or their bank may decrease their original offer substantially to a point that you are not happy with. If you neglected your business bad enough and profits fell a very large amount, the buyer may even walk away from the deal completely. Now your business is hurting, and you can't find anyone to buy it.

When you finally make the decision to sell your business you may be tempted to "check out" and start focusing on other things in your life because you know you are done with your business. Do not do this. If you've made the decision to sell your business, it means that you now have a long road ahead to get to the closing table. A road that could last 12 months or even longer. You must stay focused on your business during this time that it is for sale. The sale of your business is not a sure thing until after the sale has closed! Plan a big celebration with your loved ones and friends for after your deal closes. Until then, stay focused on your business all the way to the end. Otherwise you might lose a lot of money at the closing table because the financial performance of your business decreased while it was listed for sale or worse you may lose a great buyer all together and be worse off than when you first began listing it for sale.

MISTAKE #19:
MOVING TOO FAST WITH A BUYER

There are some buyers who move too fast and make offers prematurely before they have reviewed enough information about your business. They do this because they are afraid if they don't someone else will buy your business before they can.

Why is this a problem? It is a problem because of the exclusivity clause in buyers' offers. If you accept their offer you will not be able to continue to market your business for sale, discuss your business with other potential buyers or accept offers from other buyers. This is called "exclusivity" and it is a legal requirement the buyer places on you when you accept a buyer's offer.

If you accept an offer from a buyer who is moving too fast the exclusivity clause will require you to take your business off the market for as much as 30-45 days while the buyer does their due diligence on your business. It is during this time that the buyer will finally review information that they should have reviewed before they made their offer and they may decide to either lower their offer or walk away completely.

The result is that you just lost 30-45 days of valuable time that you could have had your business on the market. You could have been receiving offers from other buyers who had reviewed all of the important information on your business and who would have given you a more reliable offer.

When you accept a buyer's offer, the buyer is not required to follow through and buy your business. The buyer will do due diligence after you accept their offer and if they discover something they do not like, they will walk away. When a buyer is moving too fast and you accept their offer, you are only benefiting the buyer and hurting yourself.

MISTAKES INVOLVING DEAL MAKING

MISTAKE #20: NOT USING AN ATTORNEY

You may be tempted to ask your business broker to write contracts for you or give you legal advice about contracts buyers write. This may seem reasonable because, after all, your business broker has a lot of experience with these types of contracts. Plus, it would be nice to save some money by not paying an attorney to do what your business broker can do.

Do not make this mistake. It is worth every penny to have your business attorney review the buyer's Offer Letter/Letter of Intent and the Purchase Agreement along with any other legal documents that are a part of your specific deal.

You can either save a small amount of money before you close the sale of your business by not having your attorney review the contracts or you can save a large amount after your business is sold by avoiding a lawsuit because you did not sign bad contracts.

Selling your business is not something you do often in your lifetime. Don't go the cheap route. It is well worth it to play it safe and use an attorney. Plus, if your business broker is a good one, they will refuse to give you legal advice because they will not want to put you at risk. Instead, a good business broker will always refer you to your attorney for legal counsel.

MISTAKE #21: MAKING THE BUYER THINK YOU NEED THEM

Your negotiation with the buyer is obviously important because it determines how much money you will get for your business and how you will be paid.

The best way to have success in a negotiation is to have the other party think that you may walk away from the deal and not come back. In other words, you want the buyer to always think that if they don't give you what you want you will simply leave and go on to the next buyer. You never want to let the buyer think that you need them.

How do you do this? How do you not let the buyer think that you need them?

The best way is to do nothing. No phone calls. No emails. No meetings. No contact of any kind. When you literally do nothing, the buyer starts to wonder. "Why haven't they called me back or replied to my email yet?"

When you do the opposite and reply to buyer communications too quickly you are showing them that you are interested. You are showing them that you need them. When you communicate or meet with buyers you also allow them to get a read on you. What you're thinking and feeling. Buyers can then use this knowledge to their advantage in a negotiation.

You should negotiate very, very slowly. At a snail's pace. Let time pass for no reason before you respond. Make the buyer start to wonder. Make them start to fear that you are losing interest and might walk away.

Whatever you do, never negotiate in real-time whether face to face, by phone, text message or quick back and forth emails. Always let time pass. And preferably even have a person in between you and the buyer such as a business broker because that gives you even more cover and mystery to leave the buyer guessing when you might walk away.

Being a strong negotiator is simple: Do nothing. Never let the buyer think that you need them.

MISTAKE #22: NOT BEING REALISTIC ABOUT YOUR DEAL STRUCTURE

When you sell your business do you expect to receive all of the money that the buyer owes you at closing? This may or may not be possible. Some of the money that the buyer owes you may be paid to you at a future date after the closing.

This is where "deal structure" comes in to play. Deal structure means how you get paid. There are different ways buyers will try to pay you:

Types of Payments Buyers Use

Payment at Closing

This is the money that the buyer pays you at closing. You may hear this called "cash at closing". You may be able to find a buyer who will agree to pay you all of the money that they owe you at the closing (an "all-cash deal"), but it is more likely that the buyer will only pay a part of what they owe you at the closing.

Seller Note/Seller Financing

A "seller note" or "seller financing" is a contract that you have with the buyer that they will pay you part or all of the money that they owe you in the future over an agreed upon period of time. You are essentially functioning as a bank for the buyer. You and the buyer agree to an interest rate, the length of time it will take for you to be paid in full and how often the buyer makes payments. The contract that you have with the buyer stipulates that the buyer is obligated to make their payments regardless of how the business performs after they buy it.

Seller Earn Out

A "seller earn out" is a contract that you have with the buyer that they will pay you part of the money that they owe you in the future only if the business performs to certain standards after they buy it that you agree upon. If the business does not meet the standards in the future that you agreed upon, then the buyer no longer owes you the money specified in the seller earn out contract.

What Is a Realistic Deal Structure?

The truth is most buyers simply can't afford to pay you all of the money that they owe you at closing.

If this is the case, your next best bet is to do a deal structure that is a combination of cash at closing and a seller note. You want to avoid at all costs being stuck with a seller earn out as part of your deal structure. When you compare a seller note to seller earn out, the seller note does not depend on how the business performs after you leave, but the seller earn out does. No matter how capable a buyer is, you never know whether they will succeed or fail after they take over your business. For this reason, you should avoid the seller earn out if you can and try to limit your deal structure to cash at closing and a seller note if an all-cash deal is not an option.

If you are only willing to accept an all-cash deal, which means the buyer pays you all the money they owe you at closing, you may be waiting a long time to find a buyer who has the ability to do this. In fact, it may never happen. There are some buyers who can afford an all-cash deal, but they are usually medium to large size corporations or private equity firms. The majority of buyers in most situations do not fall into either of these categories.

In addition to being realistic about what the buyer can afford you also need to be realistic about how good your business is. If your business is young (2 years old or less) or if your business is struggling, most buyers will require some amount of seller financing or seller earn out even if they have enough money for an all-cash deal. Buyers require this as a way to reduce their risk in buying a young, unproven business or a business that is struggling.

Lastly, don't forget about the banks. If the buyer is using a bank to get a loan to buy your business, their bank will ultimately dictate the structure of the deal. Even if you and the buyer agree to an all-cash deal, when the buyer submits the deal to the bank the bank may require that a seller note is part of the deal or else they will refuse to fund the loan. See Mistake #23: Forgetting about banks, landlords and franchisors for more information.

MISTAKE #23: FORGETTING ABOUT BANKS, LANDLORDS AND FRANCHISORS

In some cases, it is not just you and the buyer who have to be in agreement. Depending on the buyer and your particular business there may also be a bank, a landlord or even a franchisor who has to agree.

Forgetting About Banks

You and the buyer may agree on a price for your business and also how the price will be paid in terms of cash at closing versus seller financing. Do not forget that the buyer's bank may not agree.

If the buyer is getting a loan to buy your business, their bank will have the final say when it comes to how much money they are willing to loan the buyer and the bank may also require you to contribute a certain amount of seller financing even if you do not want to. The bank may also require the buyer to contribute a certain amount of their own cash as a down payment at the closing and the buyer may not have that much cash.

This is why it is critical to screen buyers closely before you decide to spend time on them. You need to make sure they are financially qualified.

Also, don't have your heart set on a price and a deal structure until the bank has fully reviewed the financial data for your business.

The bank will do due diligence on your business just as much as the buyer does if not more so. In fact, the bank will get your tax return transcripts straight from the IRS by having you sign a Form 4506-T.

Whether you like it not, if the buyer is using a bank, the bank will be the one calling the shots. Sure, as the seller you can walk away from the buyer if you do not like the bank's terms, but you better be sure you can find another buyer who could do better. If not, there is nothing you can do...if you want to sell you have to accept the terms of the buyer's bank.

Forgetting About Landlords

If your business rents real estate that is essential to the ongoing success of your business, then your landlord will have to approve a lease to the buyer. If your landlord does not approve a lease to the buyer and there is no other real estate the buyer could move your business to or if you still have time left on your current lease, then your landlord has effectively killed your potential deal with that buyer.

But what if there is a transfer clause in your current lease? You should consult with your attorney regarding this question. You may find out that in practice that transfer clause does not help you--that ultimately your landlord still has the final say. But, again, this is a question for your attorney.

If you are thinking about selling your business, you should speak with your landlord to find out if they are willing to lease to a buyer and what requirements they have that the buyer will need to satisfy.

Forgetting About Franchisors

If your business is a franchise, your franchisor will need to approve the transfer of the franchise to the buyer. This means that the franchisor will review the buyer's financial data and qualifications and also meet with the buyer before approving the transfer. If the franchisor is not satisfied with the buyer, they won't approve the transfer of the franchise.

If you are thinking of selling your franchise, you should speak with your franchisor to find out what requirements they have that the buyer will need to satisfy in order for them to approve the transfer of the franchise. Knowing your franchisor's requirements, especially financial ones, will help you screen buyers at the very beginning before you spend time on them to make sure they at least satisfy the financial requirements of the franchisor.

Also, beware that your franchisor may charge a franchise transfer fee, which may or may not be substantial relative to the total size of your deal with the buyer. You and the buyer may want to keep the franchise transfer fee in mind as you consider the total purchase price and structure of your deal together.

MISTAKE #24: ALLOWING A NEGATIVE SURPRISE TO OCCUR IN DUE DILIGENCE

After you sign to accept the buyer's offer, due diligence will start. Due diligence is usually a 30-45 day period when the buyer reviews just about all of the information of your business.

They will review the tax returns for your business, the bank statements for your business, your payroll records and much more. If the buyer sees something they don't like in due diligence—a "negative surprise"—they can lower their original offer or even walk away from the deal all together.

Before you accept a buyer's offer you need to ask yourself: "Is this buyer already aware of all of the negative things that they will see about my business in due diligence?"

If the answer to this question is no, there is absolutely no point in accepting that buyer's offer and moving forward. Even though it might feel good to you to sign to accept a really great offer, it is meaningless because there is no way that offer will hold up once the buyer sees the negative surprise in due diligence.

Not only will that great offer disappear, but the buyer may actually get mad that you did not make them aware of the negative things before they spent their time writing an offer and doing due diligence and they may walk away from the deal all together and never return because you may have broken their trust.

Make all of your bad news known to the buyer before you accept their offer and enter into due diligence with them. Doing this is not just better for the buyer, it is also better for you.

MISTAKE #25: THINKING IT'S A DONE DEAL

A buyer made you an offer and you accepted it, so it's a done deal, right?

Wrong.

There can still be a lot that has to happen in order to close the deal. Here are some examples:

- Buyer does due diligence
- Buyer's bank does due diligence
- Stock or Asset Purchase Agreement
- Non-Compete Agreement
- Owner Transition Employment Agreement
- Environmental Inspection
- Equipment Inspection
- Franchisor Approval
- Landlord Approval

Disagreements between you and the buyer can arise even after you accept a buyer's offer. For example, the buyer may uncover information during due diligence that they did not expect, and they may lower their original offer.

Do not make the mistake of thinking your deal is a sure thing just because you accepted a buyer's offer.

You do not want to start making personal or family plans assuming you will be getting the proceeds from the sale of your business in case the deal falls apart.

You also do not want to prematurely tell your employees you are selling your business right after you accept a buyer's offer. At a minimum you should wait until further along in due diligence when the likelihood of closing the deal is greater.

Finally, make sure you do not "take your foot off the gas pedal" of the running of your business in case your deal falls apart after you accept the buyer's offer. If you do, your business will suffer because of your neglect. The next buyer that comes along may make you a lower offer than the original buyer because you neglected your business, the financial performance suffered and now your business is worth less.

Above all, always remember that a deal is never a sure thing until after it closes!

MISTAKES INVOLVING BUSINESS BROKERS

MISTAKE #26: NOT UNDERSTANDING THE ROLE OF YOUR BUSINESS BROKER

It is important to have a right understanding of what the role of your business broker should be. If you are not familiar with what your business broker should and should not do, there is a good chance you will end up frustrated and you may even end up hurting yourself.

What Your Business Broker Should Do

Your business broker's job is to do two things for you:

1. Find a good buyer for your business
2. Work to bring you and the buyer in agreement and keep you in agreement

These are the only things that your business broker should be doing for you.

Your business broker should have the ability to find buyers not just in your local area, but also regionally and nationwide. Your broker should be an expert at screening buyers to make sure they are qualified before you spend your valuable time talking to them.

Your broker should also be an expert intermediary and have the ability to get you and the buyer on the same page when it comes to what your business is worth and how your deal should be structured. Then as due diligence unfolds and contracts are written your broker should be able to keep you and the buyer on the same page if any disagreements arise.

What Your Business Broker Should Not Do

Here are some things that you may think your business broker should do, which they should not do:

Create your financial statements

Yes, your broker should be able to understand and explain your financial statements to buyers. However, they should not create your financial statements for you.

Creating your financial statements should be done by you or your CPA. If your broker does this, they are in a conflict of interest because they make money if your business sells and your business is more likely to sell if your financial statements are positive. So, when a buyer asks who made your financial statements and you say your broker did, the buyer will have doubts about whether or not your financial statements are true or if your broker made the statements in a way that was false so that they would be positive so that the buyer would buy the business.

Write contracts or give you legal advice

A good business broker will refer you to an attorney for legal advice and contract writing. If your business broker is willing to do these things for you, they shouldn't be because they are putting you at risk. See Mistake #20: Not using an attorney for more information.

Advise you on personal tax matters

Your business broker most likely does not stay up to date on all the changes to IRS tax codes. Therefore, they are not qualified to advise you on personal tax matters related to the sale of your business. Plus, you should have already been advised by your CPA on personal tax matters related to the sale of your business before you began the process of contacting a business broker and putting your business on the market for sale. See Mistake #8: Not doing personal tax planning before you list for business for sale for more information.

Now that you have a proper understanding of the role of your business broker you will have a smoother, less stressful selling process and you will avoid potentially harming yourself by having your business broker do things on your behalf that they are not qualified to be doing.

MISTAKE #27:
NOT USING A BUSINESS BROKER

Do you have to use a business broker to sell your business? No, you do not.

Should you use a business broker to sell your business? For most of you the answer is yes.

Remember business brokers serve two functions: Find a good buyer for your business and bring you and the buyer into agreement and keep you in agreement.

Finding a buyer for your business takes a lot of time. It takes a lot of time to do a good job screening potential buyers. If you attempt to do all this yourself and still run your business, your business will most likely suffer because there is only so much time in the day. If your business suffers then you will probably not get as much money as you could have when you finally sell it. Remember from Mistake #17: Thinking your business will sell quickly, it can take 12 months or longer to sell a profitable business.

Even if you do not need to find a buyer for your business because you already have a short list of candidates you still may need a business broker to bring you and the buyer into agreement. It is true that you could speak directly with the buyer in order to get into an agreement together, but what if you and the buyer don't see eye to eye on everything? You need a third party who is on your side to help work through these differences and build trust between you and the buyer so that you can do a deal together. In this scenario you should be able to find a business broker to work on your behalf at a substantially reduced commission rate since you have already done half of the broker's job by finding the buyers.

MISTAKE #28: NOT INTERVIEWING MULTIPLE BUSINESS BROKERS

You should interview at least 2-3 business brokers before deciding which broker to use. Even if a friend has highly recommended a business broker to you, you should still interview them along with 1-2 others. In most states, there is no licensing for business brokers. Business brokers can be very different from one to the next. There are good brokers, bad brokers and brokers that are just OK. In order to find the good brokers, you need to interview at least 2-3 of them.

How do you interview a business broker? There are many questions you can ask business brokers, which I will list in a moment. But first you need to understand what the most important qualities in a broker are.

Most Important Business Broker Qualities

Trust

By far, the most important quality you are looking for in a business broker is trust. If you can't reasonably trust your business broker, you should not be in a contract with them. Your business broker deals directly with potential buyers and is in a position to either make you a lot of money or lose a lot of your potential money in the form of proceeds from the sale of your business. Trust is the most important element in your relationship with your business broker.

Competence

Obviously your business broker needs to be competent. So, let's be specific:

Financial competency

Businesses are bought and sold primarily on the basis of past financial performance. Therefore, your business broker should be an expert at analyzing and explaining the financial statements for any business.

Ability to find quality buyers

Your business broker should be able to find buyers for their clients' businesses not just locally, but also regionally and nationwide. Your broker should also be an expert at screening potential buyers to ensure that you only spend your valuable time engaging with buyers that are highly qualified.

Excellent intermediary skills

Your business broker should have the ability to bring you and the buyer into an agreement and keep you in agreement through the closing of the sale of your business. One of the ways to assess if the broker you are interviewing has this ability is to pay particular attention to whether or not the broker is really listening to your concerns and how much he or she is able to clearly address your concerns in a way that is helpful to you. If the broker you are interviewing can do this, then they will most likely be able to do it also when it comes to bringing you and the buyer into agreement and keeping you in agreement.

As you can see, when you interview business brokers you are looking for signs of trust and competence. Now, let's take a look at some of the questions that are good to ask in order to help you assess the broker's trust and competence.

Business Broker Interview Questions

What is the most important part of what you do?

What do you care about the most when it comes to working with clients?

How fast do you usually respond to communications from your clients?

How selective are you? What percentage of potential sellers do you usually turn away?

Please explain the selling process to me in detail.

Would you be willing to do a free, no obligations valuation on my business?

What are your thoughts on the financial statements for my business?

In your opinion, is my business sellable?

What are the biggest obstacles that you see in getting my business sold?

How long do you think it will take to sell my business?

Where will you find buyers for my business?

What types of buyers does your firm usually find?

How do you screen buyers?

How do you decide which buyers are worth spending time on?

What would you say if a buyer asks for seller financing?

Do you have SBA lender contacts that you can refer buyers to if needed?

Do you have all buyers sign an NDA before sharing information about my business with them?

Can I see a copy of the NDA or Confidentiality Agreement that you have buyers sign before giving them information about my business?

How much and what kind of information about my business do you usually recommend sharing with buyers and when?

What kinds of things do buyers ask to see before due diligence?

What kinds of things do buyers ask to see during due diligence?

How long does due diligence usually last?

What is the most important thing about a negotiation to you?

What do you do to be a strong negotiator?

What will you do to make sure that I am always in a position of strength in a negotiation?

How fast do you usually respond to communications from buyers?

What are your commission rates?

Besides your commission, are there any other costs or fees I will need to pay you?

Do I pay you anything if you do not sell my business?

Can I see a copy of the contract you would use between us?

Can I exclude firms or individuals from the contract that we will have between us so that I can sell my business to these firms or individuals at any point during the term of our contract without having to pay you a commission should I choose to do so?

Do you have a business attorney that you recommend?

Do you have a closing attorney that you recommend?

Do you have a CPA that you recommend?

MISTAKE #29: FORGETTING THAT A GOOD BUSINESS BROKER IS ALSO INTERVIEWING YOU

When you are interviewing business brokers don't forget the fact that the good brokers will also be interviewing you. A good broker will be interviewing you in two ways:

Assessing the Quality of Your Business

A good business broker will assess the quality of your business. They will do this by carefully reviewing your financial statements and the tax returns for your business before they agree to take your business to the marketplace so that they can verify that your business is indeed sellable. See Mistake #7: Not accepting that your business is unsellable for more information.

Assessing the Potential for a Productive Working Relationship

The business broker-client relationship is similar to a business partnership. Good brokers are able to determine fairly quickly what you would be like to work with as a partner on the goal of selling your business. A good broker determines this by assessing: Your trustworthiness; whether or not you follow through and do what you say you are going to do; how organized you are when it comes to running your business; how you respond to difficult questions that the broker asks you and how realistic your expectations are for selling your business.

The best policy to follow in your initial conversations with business brokers is to give honest, straightforward answers to their questions and provide them with all of the financial information that they request. This will allow the broker to give you realistic feedback and let you know their opinion on where you really stand, which is what is going to be the most helpful to you as you start on the path to selling your business.

MISTAKE #30: THINKING A GOOD BROKER WILL BE ABLE TO SELL A BAD COMPANY

Is your business struggling and you would like to get out of it? If so, you may be tempted to think that using a business broker will add instant credibility to your business in the minds of buyers and get your business sold.

This is not the case.

If your business is struggling or is simply not sellable, hiring a good business broker will not change that. The truth about your company's situation will come to light as buyers begin to dig. There is nothing that even the best business brokers can do about this.

It is important to remember that businesses sell themselves. The financial statements and tax returns for your business speak for themselves. There is nothing that a business broker can say or do to overcome this fact.

If you expect that a business broker can get your business sold without ever showing the buyer your financial statements, keep dreaming. The reality is business brokers won't even take your business to the marketplace if you are not willing to show buyers your financial statements.

MISTAKE #31: GETTING INTO A CONTRACT WITH A BUSINESS BROKER LONGER THAN 12 MONTHS

Some business brokers will try to get you to sign a 2-year contract. Don't do it.

They will ask you to sign a 2-year contract because it is possible that it can take longer than 12 months to sell a profitable business. It is true that it actually could end up taking 18 or even 24 months to sell a great, profitable business. How long it will take to sell a business can be hard to predict.

Even though all of this is true, it is still not necessary to bind yourself in a contract with a business broker for longer than 12 months. The reason is that the broker contract always has what is called the "tail", which covers the broker for an additional 1-2 years after the contract ends for any buyer candidate the broker brought to you. This tail ensures that the broker is not harmed if they have a candidate that is close to submitting an offer on your business towards the end of the 12th month of a 12-month contract.

If you are satisfied with the broker's performance at the 12-month mark you can renew the contract for an additional 6-12 months if you desire.

Broker contracts are exclusive which means you can only sell your business through that broker. You do not want to bind yourself to a broker for longer than 12 months in the event that you find out through the course of working together that the broker is not as good as you thought.

One more thing about business broker contracts: You can exclude firms or individuals from the contract that you have with the business broker so that you can sell your business to these firms or individuals at any point during the term of your contract without paying the broker a commission should you choose to do so. For example, if a family member, friend or acquaintance has expressed an interest in buying your business in the past, you can exclude them from your contract with your business broker so that you will not have to pay your broker a commission if you sell to any of those people. Remember, your contract with the business broker is exclusive so if you sell to anyone else during the term of the contract you will have to pay the business broker the commission stated in the contract.

MISTAKE #32: PAYING A BUSINESS BROKER TOO MUCH MONEY

Some brokers will say their standard commission rate is 12%. That is too high.

The highest commission you should pay a business broker is 10% and your goal should actually be to pay no higher than 8%.

If your business is worth more than $1 million, you should receive an additional discount for each additional million after the first $1 million down to a minimum commission rate you and the broker agree on.

For example, if your business is worth $4.5 million, the commission might be 8% on the first $1 million, 7% on the second million, 6% on the third million and then 5% on the remaining $1.5 million because you and your broker agreed that 5% would be the minimum commission rate.

Despite what you may have been told, there is not a standard commission structure in the business broker industry. All of it is up for negotiation between you and the broker. You should "shop around" by interviewing different brokers, compare their commission structures and then negotiate for the best deal you can get. As you do this remember that 10% is the absolute most you should pay, and you should try to get it down to 8%. If your business is worth more than $1 million, you should negotiate aggressively for additional discounts on commission rates for the portions of the purchase price above $1 million.

You can also provide your broker with a list of potential buyers that you would like your broker to solicit, such as your competitors. The commission rates on that list of buyers should be 50% less than the rates I described above because you have done half of the broker's job for them by finding the qualified buyers that are on that list. The caveat is that you need to be able to make the case to your broker why the buyers on this list are likely to have a serious strategic interest in acquiring your business. Some examples of the kind of case you need to make include: You have already started a conversation with the buyer about acquiring your business; the buyer has expressed an interest in acquiring your business in the past; you know the buyer personally; the buyer does the same thing as you in a different geographic area and wants to expand to your area; the buyer is familiar with your clients and employees and would like to expand by acquiring you; etc. On the other hand, if you give your broker a long list of companies in your industry without making a case as to why each one would have a strategic reason to buy you, do not expect your broker to cut their commission rates in half.

The contract between you and your broker should set different commission rates as I have described above based on buyers that are on the list you provide to your broker versus buyers that your broker finds for you.

Lastly, always remember that you should not pay any other costs to the broker besides the commission if they sell your business. If a broker also tries to charge you a retainer for their services or additional marketing fees, look elsewhere. If your broker does not sell your business, you should pay them a grand total of $0 (zero) dollars.

CONCLUSION

Feeling overwhelmed? Don't worry, that is to be expected. And don't feel like you have to remember everything you've just read. You can use this book as a point of reference as you go through your selling process. You can always refer back to this book as often as you need to.

By now after reading this book one of the things you know is that you need to have an attorney, probably a CPA, and maybe even a business broker that are all competent and that you can trust. You will still have to look out for your own best interests, but these professionals, if they are good ones, will be a help to you in the selling process.

You also know by now how important your financial records are and that they need to be properly prepared, organized and ready to send to buyers. If this is not the case for you, do not be discouraged. You are in the same boat as many other business owners. But you do need to swallow the pill and get together with a CPA and get your financial records in order if you want to sell your business.

At the end of the day selling your business is all about trust--trust that is built between you and the buyer. When someone buys your business, they are doing so trusting that what you have said about your business is indeed true. Remember what you have learned in this book about what buyers think is valuable in a business. This will help you earn their trust and get the best deal possible for yourself.

My sincere hope is that this book has helped you and benefits you greatly when you sell your company. May you reduce your stress and have significant advantages during the process of selling your business by studying and avoiding the 32 mistakes in this book. I know you will.

ABOUT THE AUTHOR

Ben Hill is a Partner of Grayhill Business Brokers and serves as the firm's Managing Broker leading Grayhill's team of business brokers. Ben has brokered the sale of millions of dollars of businesses both large and small.

Ben has both ownership and operation experience in the small business sector across multiple industries. Ben is passionate about helping Grayhill clients reach their exit goals and making the transition to their next venture or retirement a smooth one.

Ben earned his bachelor's degree cum laude in Business Administration from Furman University where he was the recipient of the university's distinguished General Excellence in Business Award, which is a monetary prize awarded to one graduating senior each year.

When not selling businesses, Ben enjoys spending time with his wife and three kids, swimming and the family Boykin Spaniel.

Made in the USA
Middletown, DE
06 February 2022